George Washington

Written by Marcia S. Gresko
Illustrated by Sue Fullam

Mount Vernon

George Washington
lived on a farm
in Virginia.

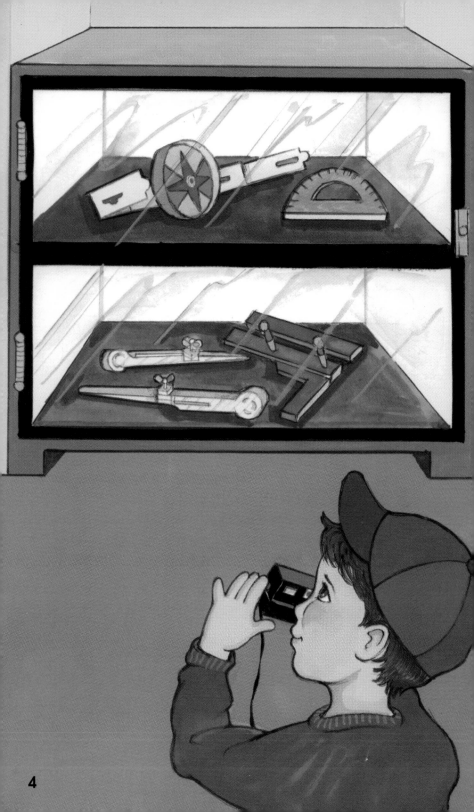

Surveyor's Tools

When George was
a young man,
he learned
to measure land
and make maps.

Martha Custis and her children, Martha and John

George married
Martha Custis.
She had two children.

Statue of Washington
in the park

George was a
brave soldier.
He led the fight for
independence.

Mount Rushmore
National Memorial,
shows Washington, Jefferson,
Roosevelt, and Lincoln

**George became
the first president
of the United States.**

The Capitol Building
in Washington, D.C.

The capital city of
the United States is
named after him.

Washington Monument

There is also a monument for him in Washington, D.C.

George Washington
is remembered as
"The Father of the Country."